My Grandmother and Me

A MEMORY SCRAPBOOK FOR KIDS

written by
JANE DRAKE and ANN LOVE

illustrated by
SCOT RITCHIE

KIDS CAN PRESS

My Grandmother and Me

My name is _____.

My grandmother's special name for me is _____.

I was born on _____ _____, _____.
                    (month)   *(day)*   *(year)*

I am _____ years old.

I was born in _____, _____.
                   (city/town)   *(country)*

I am my grandmother's

☐ oldest grandchild

☐ youngest grandchild

☐ only grandchild

☐ second grandchild

☐ _____

My grandmother's name is _____.

My special name for my grandmother is _____.

My grandmother was born on _____ _____, _____.
                                                (month)   *(day)*   *(year)*

She is _____ years old.

My grandmother was born in _____, _____.
                                      (city/town)   *(country)*

She is my ☐ mother's mother

           ☐ father's mother

           ☐ _____

Look at Us

Here's a picture of my grandmother and me together:

My grandmother and I look

- ☐ a little bit alike
- ☐ a lot alike
- ☐ nothing alike

We both have

- ☐ big feet
- ☐ glasses
- ☐ curly hair
- ☐ a crooked nose
- ☐ _____

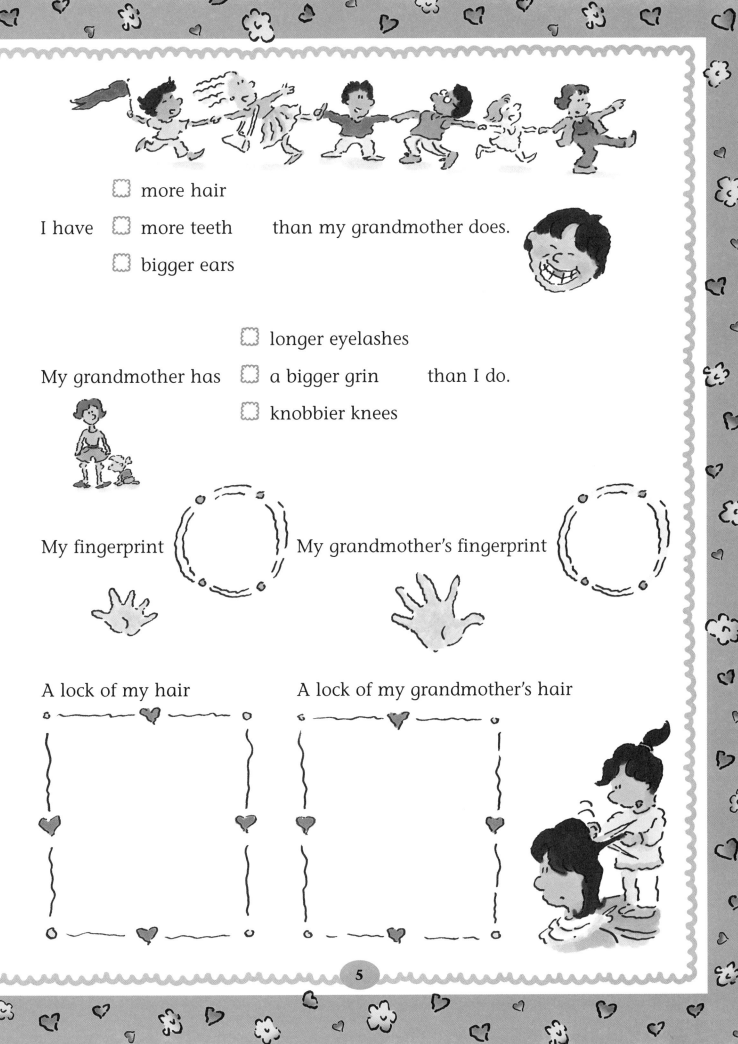

I have
☐ more hair
☐ more teeth   than my grandmother does.
☐ bigger ears

My grandmother has
☐ longer eyelashes
☐ a bigger grin   than I do.
☐ knobbier knees

My fingerprint   My grandmother's fingerprint

A lock of my hair   A lock of my grandmother's hair

Our Family Tree

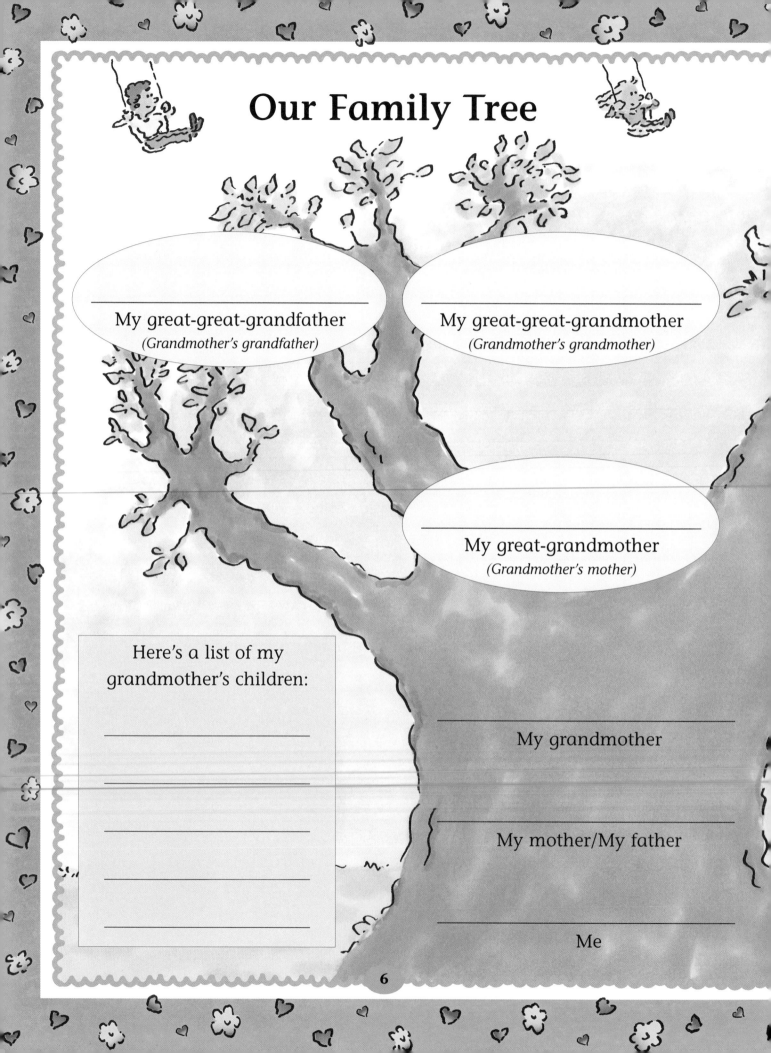

My great-great-grandfather
(Grandmother's grandfather)

My great-great-grandmother
(Grandmother's grandmother)

My great-grandmother
(Grandmother's mother)

Here's a list of my grandmother's children:

_____

_____

_____

_____

My grandmother

My mother/My father

Me

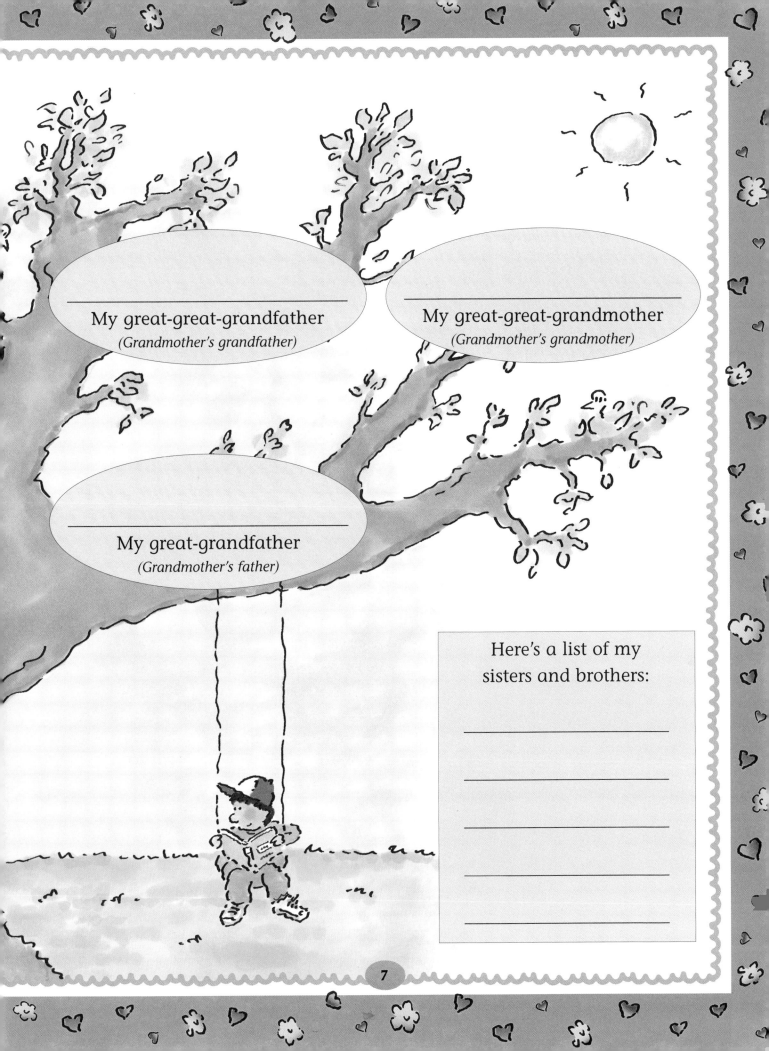

My great-great-grandfather
(Grandmother's grandfather)

My great-great-grandmother
(Grandmother's grandmother)

My great-grandfather
(Grandmother's father)

Here's a list of my
sisters and brothers:

What We're Like

I am funny

☐ sometimes

☐ all the time

☐ only when I'm at school

My grandmother is funny

☐ sometimes

☐ all the time

☐ only with her friends

I am tidy

☐ sometimes

☐ all the time

☐ only when I have to clean my room

My grandmother is tidy

☐ sometimes

☐ all the time

☐ only when company is coming

I am brave

- [ ] all the time
- [ ] sometimes
- [ ] when I watch a scary show

My grandmother is brave

- [ ] all the time
- [ ] sometimes
- [ ] when she goes to the dentist

I am bossy

- [ ] sometimes
- [ ] all the time
- [ ] only when I know I'm right

My grandmother is bossy

- [ ] sometimes
- [ ] all the time
- [ ] only when she needs to be

I would like to be _____, just like my grandmother.

My grandmother would like to be _____, just like me.

Where We Live

I live in _____, _____.
 (city/town)   *(country)*

My grandmother lives in _____, _____.
                         (city/town)   *(country)*

My home is ☐ an apartment   ☐ in the country

☐ a house   ☐ by the ocean

☐ a trailer   ☐ _____

My grandmother's home is ☐ an apartment   ☐ on a farm

☐ a house   ☐ in the city

☐ a retirement home ☐ _____

My grandmother and I live

☐ together

☐ close by

☐ far apart

This is how I get to my grandmother's *(circle the picture)*:

My grandmother's home is ⬜ cozy   ⬜ neat   ⬜ messy   ⬜ cool

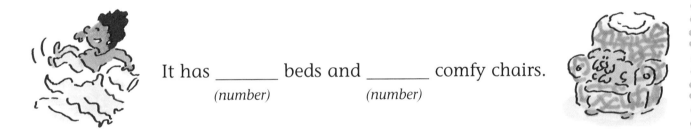

It has _____ beds and _____ comfy chairs.
(number)   *(number)*

When I visit my grandmother, I like to look at her

⬜ photographs

⬜ button box

⬜ baseball cards

⬜ rock collection

⬜ _____

Amazing Grandmother, Amazing Me

My grandmother can

☐ speak two languages

☐ fix anything

☐ bake pies

☐ sing like a bird

☐ knit warm mittens

☐ do three things at once

☐ make people laugh

☐ _____

My grandmother showed me how to

☐ thread a needle

☐ play cards

☐ tie my shoes

☐ make a birdfeeder

☐ read

☐ whistle

☐ wink

☐ _____

The most amazing thing about my grandmother is

_____.

Z Y X W V U T S R !!!

I can

- ☐ skate
- ☐ draw great pictures
- ☐ speak two languages
- ☐ score a goal
- ☐ say the alphabet backward
- ☐ touch my nose with my tongue
- ☐ catch a fish
- ☐ _____

I showed my grandmother how to

- ☐ wiggle her ears
- ☐ do a somersault
- ☐ use a computer
- ☐ catch a frog
- ☐ eat spaghetti
- ☐ find the Big Dipper
- ☐ make a funny face
- ☐ _____

My grandmother thinks I'm amazing because

_____.

Naughty and Nice

The naughtiest thing I ever did was _____

_____.

After I was naughty, I looked like this *(circle the picture)*:

And I felt ⬜ scared   ⬜ sorry   ⬜ silly   ⬜ _____

The naughtiest thing my grandmother ever did was _____

_____.

After she was naughty, she looked like this *(circle the picture)*:

And she felt ⬜ sad   ⬜ scared   ⬜ silly   ⬜ _____

The nicest thing I ever did was _____

_____.

When I was nice, I looked like this *(circle the picture)*:

And I felt ☐ proud ☐ shy ☐ grown-up ☐ _____

The nicest thing my grandmother ever did was _____

_____.

After she was nice, she looked like this *(circle the picture)*:

And she felt ☐ proud ☐ shy ☐ brave ☐ _____

Our Favorite Things

Favorite Things	My List	My Grandmother's List
Color	_____	_____
Clothes	_____	_____
TV show	_____	_____
Movie	_____	_____
Song	_____	_____
Book	_____	_____
Sport	_____	_____

Favorite Things	My List	My Grandmother's List
Time of the day	_____	_____
Month	_____	_____
Season	_____	_____
Weather	_____	_____
Animal	_____	_____
Bug	_____	_____
Flower	_____	_____

What We Like to Eat

My favorite food is _____.

My grandmother's favorite food is _____.

For a special treat, my grandmother and I like to share

- ☐ pizza
- ☐ ice cream
- ☐ chocolate

- ☐ potato chips
- ☐ broccoli
- ☐ _____

My grandmother thinks the strangest food I eat is

- ☐ gummy worms
- ☐ cold spaghetti

- ☐ spinach
- ☐ _____

I think the strangest food my grandmother eats is

- ☐ sardines on toast
- ☐ snails

- ☐ tofu
- ☐ _____

My grandmother makes the best

 macaroni

 bread

 cookies

 soup

☐ _____

Our favorite food to make together is _____.

And here are some of the things we need to make it *(circle the picture)*:

19

Perfect Places

My favorite inside place is

- [ ] my bedroom
- [ ] my grandmother's attic
- [ ] a barn
- [ ] _____

My grandmother's favorite inside place is

- [ ] a kitchen
- [ ] a gym
- [ ] a museum
- [ ] _____

My favorite outside place is

- [ ] a tree house
- [ ] the beach
- [ ] an amusement park
- [ ] _____

My grandmother's favorite outside place is

- [ ] a garden
- [ ] a campground
- [ ] her neighborhood
- [ ] _____

If my grandmother and I could go anywhere together,

we'd go to _____.

When we got there, the first thing we'd do is

_____.

Then we would go to visit _____.

We would eat lots of _____.

Here's a picture of what we'd bring home as a souvenir:

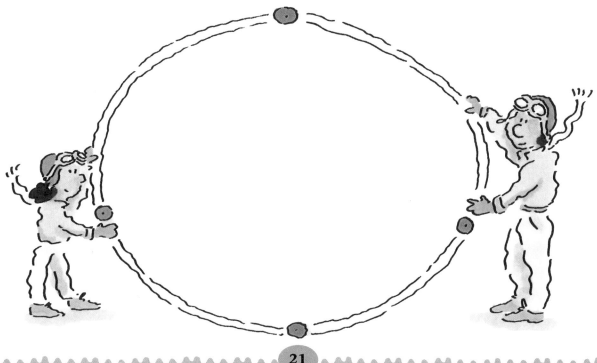

Holidays and Celebrations

My grandmother and I celebrate special days together.

Our favorite time to celebrate is

- ☐ our birthdays
- ☐ the New Year
- ☐ Passover
- ☐ Christmas
- ☐ Eid
- ☐ Kwanzaa
- ☐ Thanksgiving
- ☐ _____

The best part of our celebration is _____.

We eats lots of _____.

We wear _____.

When we can't celebrate together, we

- ☐ phone each other
- ☐ send cards
- ☐ think about each other
- ☐ _____

Here are some pictures, photographs and other special things from our celebrations together:

Looking Backward, Looking Forward

When my grandmother was my age,

she liked to go to _____.

She liked to play _____.

She liked to collect _____.

Her best friend's name was _____.

Her favorite subject in school was _____.

Her worst subject in school was _____.

She liked school
☐ every day
☐ some days
☐ _____

When I get to be my grandmother's age,

I'll go to _____.

I'll play _____.

I'll collect _____.

When I get to be my grandmother's age,

these are the things I'll tell my grandchildren.

My best friend's name was _____.

My favorite subject in school was _____.

My worst subject in school was _____.

I liked school
⬚ every day
⬚ some days
⬚ _____

When We're Together

These are some of the things my grandmother and I like to do together:

- [ ] walk and talk
- [ ] swim
- [ ] read books

- [ ] knit
- [ ] ride horses
- [ ] play ball

- [ ] visit friends
- [ ] sing
- [ ] _____

Here's a picture of my grandmother and me
doing our favorite thing together:

These are some of the places my grandmother and I go together:

- [ ] the movie theater
- [ ] the museum
- [ ] the seashore
- [ ] the city
- [ ] the library
- [ ] the mountains
- [ ] the fall fair
- [ ] the cottage
- [ ] _____
- [ ] the skating rink
- [ ] the park
- [ ] _____

Here are some souvenirs I've collected on my trips with my grandmother:

When We're Apart

When we're apart, lots of things remind me of my grandmother.

Especially when I smell
- ☐ roses
- ☐ rain
- ☐ fresh bread
- ☐ _____

Especially when I hear
- ☐ a bird singing
- ☐ a thunderstorm
- ☐ rock and roll
- ☐ _____

Especially when I see
- ☐ the sun rising
- ☐ a kite flying
- ☐ her photograph
- ☐ _____

Especially when I
- ☐ sit under a tree
- ☐ feel happy
- ☐ score a goal
- ☐ _____

When we're apart, lots of things remind my grandmother of me.

Especially when she smells

☐ apples

☐ running shoes

☐ bubble bath

☐ _____

Especially when she hears

☐ kids playing

☐ a train

☐ the ocean

☐ _____

Especially when she sees

☐ balloons

☐ a soccer ball

☐ a ballerina

☐ _____

Our Special Stories

My grandmother tells me stories about when she was growing up.

Her stories are about

- ☐ funny things her family did
- ☐ where she used to live
- ☐ exciting adventures she had

- ☐ her secret hiding places
- ☐ things she'll never forget
- ☐ _____

Here is one of my grandmother's special stories.

_____

_____

_____

_____

My grandmother likes to tell this story about me.

_____

_____

_____

_____

I tell stories too. I tell my grandmother stories about

- ☐ funny things I've done
- ☐ my daydreams
- ☐ my most exciting adventures

- ☐ the best time I ever had
- ☐ my secret hiding places
- ☐ _____

Here is one of my special stories.

_____

_____

_____

_____

I like to tell this story about my grandmother.

_____

_____

_____

_____

Dedicated to a wonderful Nanny, Marjorie Snowden — JD & AL
To my grandmothers — SR

Published in Canada by
Kids Can Press Ltd.
29 Birch Avenue
Toronto, ON M4V 1E2

Published in the U.S. by
Kids Can Press Ltd
85 River Rock Drive, Suite 202
Buffalo, NY 14207

Edited by Tara Walker and Linda Biesenthal
Designed by Julia Naimska

Printed in Hong Kong by Wing King Tong Co. Ltd.

CM 99 0 9 8 7 6 5 4 3 2 1

ISBN 1-55074-628-6

Kids Can Press is a Nelvana company.